DINOSAUR FACT DIG

IGUANODON

AND OTHER BIRD-FOOTED DINOSAURS

THE NEED-TO-KNOW FACTS

BY

JANET RIEHECKY

Consultant: Mathew J. Wedel, PhD
Associate Professor
Western University of Health Services

raintree
a Capstone company — publishers for children

Raintree is an imprint of Capstone Global Library Limited, a company incorporated in England and Wales having its registered office at 264 Banbury Road, Oxford, OX2 7DY - Registered company number: 6695582

www.raintree.co.uk
myorders@raintree.co.uk

Text © Capstone Global Library Limited 2017
The moral rights of the proprietor have been asserted.

EDITORIAL CREDITS
Michelle Hasselius, editor; Kazuko Collins, designer; Wanda Winch, media researcher; Gene Bentdahl, production specialist

ISBN 978 1 474 7 2824 9
20 19 18 17 16
10 9 8 7 6 5 4 3 2 1

British Library Cataloguing in Publication Data
A full catalogue record for this book is available from the British Library.

ACKNOWLEDGEMENTS
All images by Jon Hughes except: MapArt (maps), Shutterstock: Elena Elisseeva, green gingko leaf, Jiang Hongyan, yellow gingko leaf, Taigi, paper background

We would like to thank Dr Mathew J. Wedel for his invaluable help in the preparation of this book.

Every effort has been made to contact copyright holders of material reproduced in this book. Any omissions will be rectified in subsequent printings if notice is given to the publisher.

All the internet addresses (URLs) given in this book were valid at the time of going to press. However, due to the dynamic nature of the internet, some addresses may have changed, or sites may have changed or ceased to exist since publication. While the author and publisher regret any inconvenience this may cause readers, no responsibility for any such changes can be accepted by either the author or the publisher.

Printed and bound in China.

CONTENTS

Iguanodon and other bird-footed dinosaurs were herbivores that used their hard beaks and teeth to eat plants. Dinosaurs in this group could walk on two legs. But they could also drop down on all four legs to eat low-growing plants.

Bird-footed dinosaurs did not have long claws or armour to protect them. Instead many dinosaurs in this group ran away from predators. These dinosaurs also lived in herds. Predators were less likely to attack a large group of dinosaurs. Read on to learn more about Iguanodon and other bird-footed dinosaurs.

ABRICTOSAURUS

PRONOUNCED: ab-RICK-toh-SAWR-us

NAME MEANING: wide-awake lizard

TIME PERIOD LIVED: Early Jurassic Period

LENGTH: 1.2 metres (4 feet)

WEIGHT: 41 to 45 kilograms
(90 to 100 pounds)

TYPE OF EATER: herbivore

PHYSICAL FEATURES: long tail;
large hands; sharp, pointed beak

ABRICTOSAURUS was one of
the first dinosaurs found that had
different kinds of teeth in its mouth.

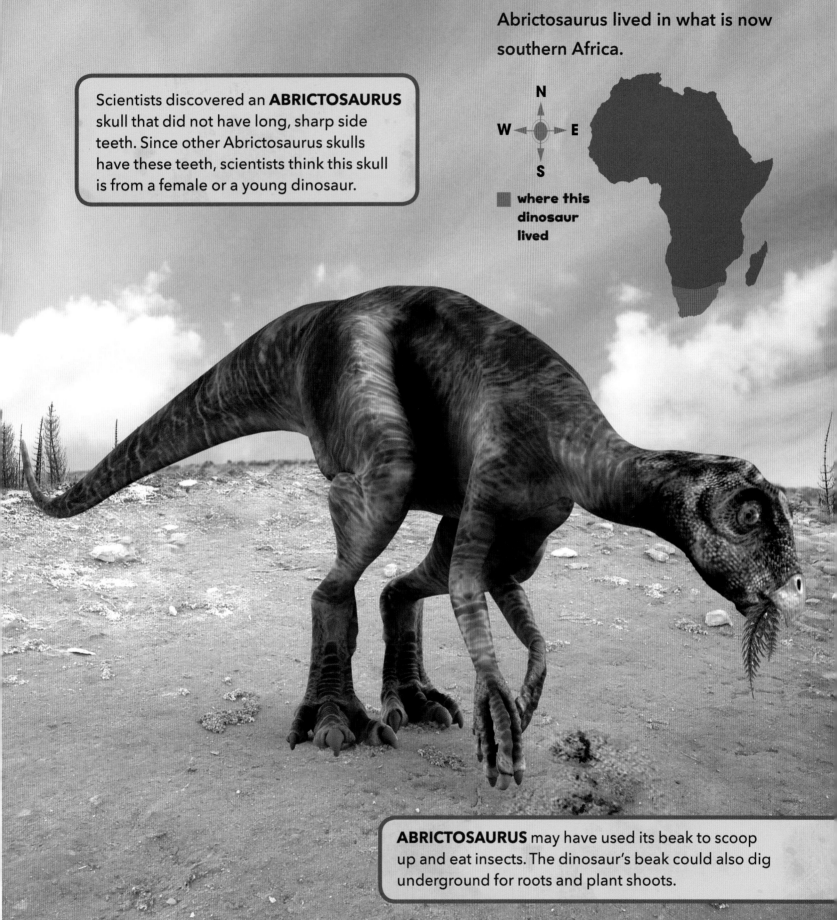

Scientists discovered an **ABRICTOSAURUS** skull that did not have long, sharp side teeth. Since other Abrictosaurus skulls have these teeth, scientists think this skull is from a female or a young dinosaur.

Abrictosaurus lived in what is now southern Africa.

N
W — E
S

■ where this dinosaur lived

ABRICTOSAURUS may have used its beak to scoop up and eat insects. The dinosaur's beak could also dig underground for roots and plant shoots.

GASPARINISAURA

PRONOUNCED: GAS-pih-RIN-ih-SAWR-uh

NAME MEANING: Gasparini's lizard; named after paleontologist Zulma Brandoni de Gasparini

TIME PERIOD LIVED: Late Cretaceous Period

LENGTH: 0.6 metres (2.1 feet)

WEIGHT: 2.3 kilograms (5 pounds)

TYPE OF EATER: herbivore

PHYSICAL FEATURES: long, thick tail; long feet; short head

GASPARINISAURA swallowed rocks to help it digest plants. The rocks helped break down the plants into tiny pieces.

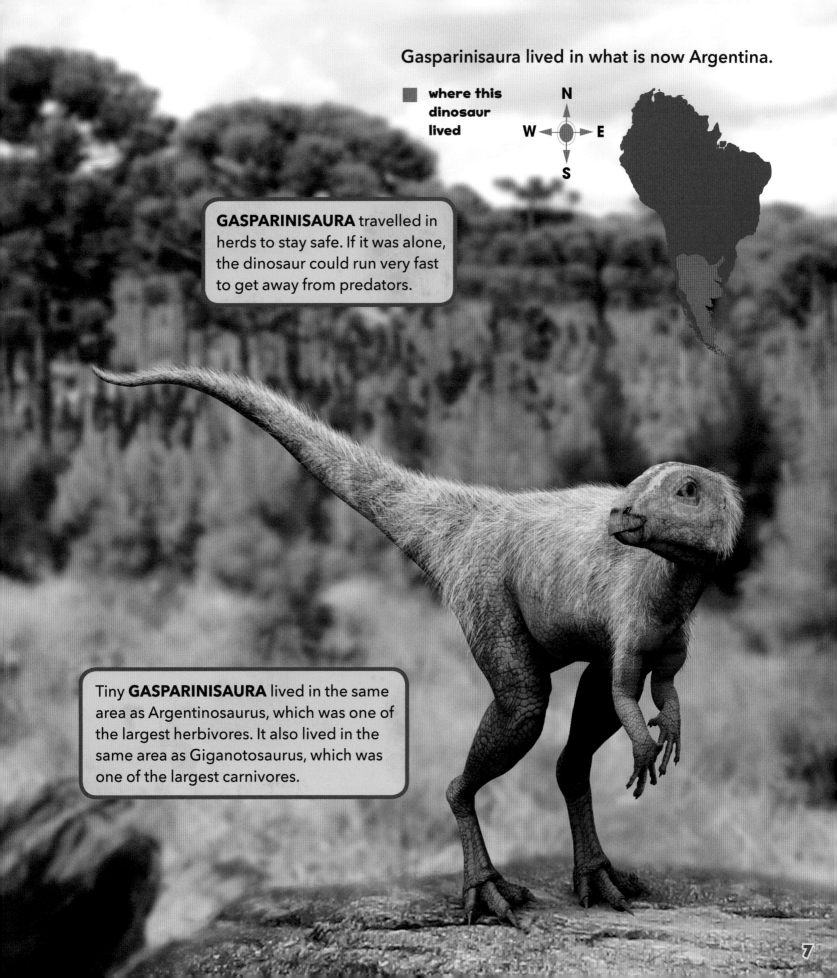

Gasparinisaura lived in what is now Argentina.

■ where this dinosaur lived

N
W ← ✦ → E
S

GASPARINISAURA travelled in herds to stay safe. If it was alone, the dinosaur could run very fast to get away from predators.

Tiny **GASPARINISAURA** lived in the same area as Argentinosaurus, which was one of the largest herbivores. It also lived in the same area as Giganotosaurus, which was one of the largest carnivores.

HEXINLUSAURUS

PRONOUNCED: HEX-in-luh-SAWR-us

NAME MEANING: named after Professor He Xin-Lu from the Chengdu University of Technology in China

TIME PERIOD LIVED: Middle Jurassic Period

LENGTH: 1.8 metres (6 feet)

WEIGHT: 9 to 23 kilograms (20 to 50 pounds)

TYPE OF EATER: herbivore

PHYSICAL FEATURES: thick tail; long legs; short arms

Hexinlusaurus lived in an area with shallow lakes in what is now central China.

■ where this dinosaur lived

Scientists had a hard time deciding what kind of dinosaur **HEXINLUSAURUS** was. They thought its fossils could be from Yangdusaurus, Agilisaurus and Proyandusaurus.

HEXINLUSAURUS' fossils are at the Zigong Dinosaur Museum in Dashanpu, China.

Scientists have only found HEXINLUSAURUS' skull and a few bones so far.

HYPSILOPHODON

PRONOUNCED: HIP-sih-LOF-uh-don

NAME MEANING: high-ridged tooth

TIME PERIOD LIVED: Early Cretaceous Period

LENGTH: 1.8 metres (5.9 feet)

WEIGHT: 9 to 23 kilograms (20 to 50 pounds)

TYPE OF EATER: herbivore

PHYSICAL FEATURES: five fingers on each hand; large eyes; wide, leaf-shaped teeth

Scientists have found **HYPSILOPHODON** nests with carefully arranged eggs. This might mean the dinosaur took care of its young.

At first scientists thought **HYPSILOPHODON** lived in trees. Now scientists know it lived on land.

Hypsilophodon lived near rivers, lakes and swamps in what is now western Europe and Alberta, Canada.

where this dinosaur lived

When **HYPSILOPHODON** closed its mouth, its top teeth slid over the outside of its bottom teeth like scissors. Every time the dinosaur opened or closed its mouth, it sharpened its teeth.

IGUANODON

PRONOUNCED: ih-GWAN-oh-don

NAME MEANING: iguana tooth

TIME PERIOD LIVED: Early Cretaceous Period

LENGTH: 9 metres (30 feet)

WEIGHT: 3.2 metric tons (3.5 tons)

TYPE OF EATER: herbivore

PHYSICAL FEATURES: stiff tail used for balance; sharp spikes for thumbs; leaf-shaped teeth

At first scientists thought **IGUANODON** had a spike on its nose. Now scientists know it had spikes instead of thumbs. The dinosaur could use its thumb spikes to stab at food or to protect itself.

Close relatives of **IGUANODON** have been found in North America, Africa, Asia and Australia.

IGUANODON was the second dinosaur to be named.

IGUANODON had teeth on the sides of its mouth. The dinosaur could use these teeth to chew up plants.

IGUANODON became extinct about 125 million years ago.

IGUANODON could walk on two or four legs, similar to a kangaroo today.

Iguanodon lived in woodlands in what is now Europe.

IGUANODON was discovered in 1822. The dinosaur's giant teeth were stuck in rocks near Sussex, England.

N
W E
S

■ where this dinosaur lived

LEAELLYNASAURA

PRONOUNCED: lee-EL-in-a-SAWR-ah

NAME MEANING: Leaellyn's lizard; named after the daughter of paleontologists Patricia Vickers-Rich and Thomas Rich

TIME PERIOD LIVED: Early Cretaceous Period

LENGTH: 0.9 metres (3 feet)

WEIGHT: 2 to 9 kilograms (5 to 20 pounds)

TYPE OF EATER: herbivore

PHYSICAL FEATURES: very long tail; bone that stuck out above eyes; huge eyes

LEAELLYNASAURA lived in a place that got very cold during the winter. The Sun did not come up for three months. Some scientists think this means the dinosaur was warm-blooded.

LEAELLYNASAURA had huge eyes. Some scientists think the dinosaur could see in the dark.

Leaellynasaura lived in forests in what is now southern Australia.

where this dinosaur lived

LEAELLYNASAURA had better eyesight than any other dinosaur in this group.

MUTTABURRASAURUS

PRONOUNCED: MUT-uh-BUR-uh-SAWR-us

NAME MEANING: named after the town of Muttaburra in Australia, where fossils were found

TIME PERIOD LIVED: Early Cretaceous Period

LENGTH: 9 metres (29.5 feet)

WEIGHT: 0.9 to 3.6 metric tons (1 to 4 tons)

TYPE OF EATER: herbivore

PHYSICAL FEATURES: long tail; powerful jaw; sharp teeth; long, rounded nose

MUTTABURRASAURUS had a large, hollow space inside its nose. Some scientists think the space helped the dinosaur to smell. Others think the dinosaur used it to make loud sounds.

Muttaburrasaurus lived in conifer forests in what is now Australia.

N
W — E
S

■ where this dinosaur lived

Scientists made casts of **MUTTABURRASAURUS'** bones and put them together. It was the first Australian dinosaur to be put on display.

Humans and most animals lose one tooth at a time. **MUTTABURRASAURUS** lost a whole row of teeth. A new row of teeth was waiting underneath to replace it.

ORYCTODROMEUS

PRONOUNCED: or-ICK-toh-DROH-me-us

NAME MEANING: digging runner

TIME PERIOD LIVED: middle Cretaceous Period

LENGTH: 2 metres (7 feet)

WEIGHT: 23 to 45 kilograms (50 to 100 pounds)

TYPE OF EATER: herbivore

PHYSICAL FEATURES: tail that bent easily; strong legs; powerful shoulder muscles; broad, horned beak

ORYCTODROMEUS took care of its young until they were fully grown.

Oryctodromeus lived in dry woodlands in what is now Montana, USA.

N
W   E
S

where this dinosaur lived

ORYCTODROMEUS dug underground burrows to lay its eggs. The eggs would be safe from dangerous weather and predators that couldn't fit inside.

Scientists found small side tunnels connected to **ORYCTODROMEUS'** underground burrows. This shows that insects or other small creatures shared the dinosaur's burrows.

OURANOSAURUS

PRONOUNCED: oo-RAN-oh-SAWR-us

NAME MEANING: brave lizard

TIME PERIOD LIVED: Early Cretaceous Period

LENGTH: 6 metres (19.7 feet)

WEIGHT: 0.9 to 3.6 metric tons (1 to 4 tons)

TYPE OF EATER: herbivore

PHYSICAL FEATURES: strong legs;
narrow sail on its back; small,
rounded horns; long beak

OURANOSAURUS may have been hunted
by the giant crocodile Sarchsuchus.
Sarchsuchus was almost 12 metres (40 feet)
long. Scientists nicknamed it "SuperCroc".

Ouranosaurus lived in the forests and swamps of what is now Niger in Africa.

N
W E
S

☐ where this dinosaur lived

OURANOSAURUS had thumb spikes, similar to Iguanodon.

OURANOSAURUS' sail was held up by long, wide spines. Some of the spines were almost 0.6 metres (2 feet) long.

THESCELOSAURUS

PRONOUNCED: THES-ki-loh-SAWR-us

NAME MEANING: marvellous lizard

TIME PERIOD LIVED: Late Cretaceous Period

LENGTH: 4 metres (13 feet)

WEIGHT: 227 to 272 kilograms
(500 to 600 pounds)

TYPE OF EATER: herbivore

PHYSICAL FEATURES: long, powerful legs;
wide back; short arms; small head

THESCELOSAURUS was
one of the last dinosaurs
to become extinct.

Thescelosaurus lived in what is now the northwestern United States. It also lived in southwestern Canada.

N
W · E
S

where this dinosaur lived

THESCELOSAURUS weighed about as much as a pony today.

A **THESCELOSAURUS** skeleton was found in 1993. At first scientists thought that they had found the dinosaur's fossilized heart in its chest. Later scientists discovered it was just a strange-shaped rock.

XIAOSAURUS

PRONOUNCED: ZEE-ah-oh-SAWR-us

NAME MEANING: dawn lizard

TIME PERIOD LIVED: Middle Jurassic Period

LENGTH: 0.9 metres (3 feet)

WEIGHT: 2 to 9 kilograms (5 to 20 pounds)

TYPE OF EATER: herbivore

PHYSICAL FEATURES: thin body; short arms; small claws; small head

Construction workers building a car park uncovered thousands of dinosaur bones in 1979. **XIAOSAURUS** was found in the same place four years later.

Xiaosaurus lived in what is now central China.

N
W E
S

where this
dinosaur
lived

Besides **XIAOSAURUS'** fossils, giant long-necked dinosaurs and big carnivores have been found in Dashanpu, China.

The names **XIAOSAURUS** and Eosaurus both mean "dawn lizard". Eosaurus was a reptile that lived in the sea but is now extinct.

ZEPHYROSAURUS

PRONOUNCED: ZEF-i-roh-SAWR-us

NAME MEANING: west wind lizard; Zephyros is the god of the west wind in Greek mythology

TIME PERIOD LIVED: Early Cretaceous Period

LENGTH: 1.8 metres (6 feet)

WEIGHT: 9 to 23 kilograms (20 to 50 pounds)

TYPE OF EATER: herbivore

PHYSICAL FEATURES: long tail; short arms; small head; beak

ZEPHYROSAURUS lived during the same time period as Deinonychus, a fierce raptor.

Many dinosaurs could only move their jaws up and down to chew. **ZEPHYROSAURUS** could move its jaw up and down and side to side.

Zephyrosaurus lived near the rivers and swamps of what is now western North America.

N
W E
S

■ where this dinosaur lived

ZEPHYROSAURUS may have made footprints discovered in what is now the USA, in Maryland and Virginia.

GLOSSARY

BEAK hard part of a bird's mouth; some dinosaurs had beaks

BURROW tunnel or hole in the ground made or used by an animal

CARNIVORE animal that eats only meat

CONIFER tree with cones and narrow leaves called needles

CRETACEOUS PERIOD third period of the Mesozoic Era; the Cretaceous Period was from 145 to 65 million years ago

EXTINCT no longer living; an extinct animal is one that has died out, with no more of its kind

FOSSIL remains of an animal or plant from millions of years ago that have turned to rock

HERBIVORE animal that eats only plants

HERD large group of animals that lives or travels together

HOLLOW empty on the inside

JURASSIC PERIOD second period of the Mesozoic Era; the Jurassic Period was from 200 to 145 million years ago

PALEONTOLOGIST scientist who studies fossils

PREDATOR animal that hunts other animals for food

PRONOUNCE say a word in a certain way

RELATIVE member of a family

SPIKE sharp, pointy object

SPINE backbone of an animal

WARM-BLOODED animals that have a body temperature that remains the same, no matter their surroundings; birds and mammals are warm-blooded

COMPREHENSION QUESTIONS

1. Name two dinosaurs that lived in the same area as Gasparinisaura.

2. Scientists believe Leaellynasaura could have been warm-blooded. What does "warm-blooded" mean?

3. What was unusual about the place where Xiaosaurus' bones were discovered?

READ MORE

Dinosaurs! (Knowledge Encyclopedia), DK (DK Children, 2014)

Dinosaurs in our Streets, David West (Franklin Watts, 2015)

Iguanodon (Do You Know Dinosaurs?), Helen Greathead (Scholastic, 2010)

WEBSITES

www.nhm.ac.uk/discover/dino-directory/index.html
At this Natural History Museum website you can learn more about dinosaurs through sorting them by name, country and even body shape!

www.show.me.uk/section/dinosaurs
This website has loads of fun things to do and see, including a dinosaur mask you can download and print, videos, games and Top Ten lists.

INDEX